Essential Physical Science

ELECTRICITY

Louise and Richard Spilsbury

Chicago, Illinois

Edited by Nancy Dickmann, Adam Miller,
    and Diyan Leake
Designed by Victoria Allen
Original illustrations © Capstone Global
    Library Ltd 2014
Illustrated by H L Studios
Picture research by Ruth Blair
Originated by Capstone Global Library Ltd
Printed in the United States of America in
North Mankato, Minnesota

022014
008013RP

Library of Congress Cataloging-in-Publication Data
Spilsbury, Louise
  Electricity / Louise and Richard Spilsbury.
      pages cm.—(Essential physical science)
  Includes bibliographical references and index.
  ISBN 978-1-4329-8143-3 (hb)—ISBN 978-1-4329-
8153-2 (pb) 1. Electricity—Juvenile literature. I.
Spilsbury, Richard. II. Title.
  QC527.2.S664 2014
  537—dc23   2012051622

Acknowledgments
We would like to thank the following for permission
to reproduce photographs: Alamy pp. 24 (© JoeFox
Liverpool), 27 (© Dave Pattison), 37 (© Urbanmyth),
41 (© Andrew Shurtleff); Capstone Publishers
(© Karon Dubke) pp. 14, 15, 16, 19, 22, 23, 28, 29,
34, 34, 35; Corbis pp. 17 (© Sam Sharpe/The Sharpe
Image), 26 (© Anthony Redpath), 38 (© Ocean),
42 (© Frederic Courbet); Getty Images pp. 4 (Peter
Wafzig), 5 (Robert Giroux), 6 (Oxford Scientific), 9
(Photolibrary), 12 (Fuse), 18 (JGI/Jamie Grill), 30
(Nick Veasey), 36 (Peter Anderson); © Makani Power,
A. Dunlap, 2011 p. 4; Shutterstock pp. 7 (© Violet
Kaipa), 11 (© Patrick Poendl), 13 (© Kurhan), 25
(© Kurhan), 31 (littleny), 39 (© Photoseeker), 40
(© pirita).

Cover photograph of the light trails on the
modern building background in Shanghai, China,
reproduced with permission of Shutterstock
(© zhangyang13576997233).

Every effort has been made to contact copyright
holders of material reproduced in this book. Any
omissions will be rectified in subsequent printings
if notice is given to the publisher.

Contents

What Is Electricity? 4

Where Does Electricity Come From? 6

How Do Batteries Work? 12

How Does Electricity Move? 16

What Can Electricity Flow Through? 24

How Do We Use Electricity? 30

Is Electricity Safe? 38

Electricity in the Future 42

Glossary 44

Find Out More 46

Index 48

Eureka moment!

Learn about important discoveries that have brought about further knowledge and understanding.

DID YOU KNOW?

Discover fascinating facts about electricity.

WHAT'S NEXT?

Read about the latest research and advances in essential physical science.

Some words are shown in bold, **like this**. You can find out what they mean by looking in the glossary.

What Is Electricity?

Electricity is a form of **energy** that we use to power most of the machines we use every day. It is the flow of electrical power from tiny parts called **atoms**. Everything in the world is made up of atoms, which are so small we cannot see them. Even the tiniest things have an enormous number of atoms. For example, a grain of salt has around 10 quadrillion atoms!

An atom is made of three types of parts: **protons** and **neutrons** at its center, and **electrons** that travel around them very quickly. Electricity occurs when electrons flow from atom to atom.

Then and now

Before people discovered how to make electricity, they kept warm by burning wood or coal in fireplaces. They used candles and oil lamps to light their homes and they used ice to keep food cold. Today, we use electricity to power lights, refrigerators, televisions, computers, and many other machines. We take electricity for granted—but life would be very different without it!

Electric lights and instruments help to make live rock shows loud, colorful, and exciting for huge audiences.

Eureka moment!

The ancient Greeks discovered electricity in nature about 2,500 years ago. They rubbed **amber** together with other materials and found that it produced a type of energy that attracted objects, such as feathers and cloth. Their word for amber was *electron*, and that is where we get the word *electricity* from today.

DID YOU KNOW?

In 2003, a major electricity power outage caused chaos for 50 million people in parts of the United States and Canada. In cities such as New York City and Ottawa, traffic lights and trains stopped, people were trapped in elevators, offices, and apartments, and airports closed.

Imagine your life if there were no electricity or electrical gadgets and the lights went out.

Where Does Electricity Come From?

The kind of electricity that the ancient Greeks discovered in amber is **static electricity**. Static electricity occurs in materials that rub together. It can happen when you comb your hair, because you rub some electrons off your hair and onto the comb.

Electrons produce electricity, so when the comb has more electrons and your hair has fewer electrons, static electricity pulls your hair toward the comb. When static electricity builds up, it can jump from one material to another, as a spark. Lightning is a giant spark of electricity between a cloud and the ground.

DID YOU KNOW?

There is enough electrical energy in a single flash of lightning to toast 100,000 slices of bread.

Combing your hair or rubbing a balloon on it can bring out static electricity.

How does static electricity work?

Usually, an atom has an equal number of protons and electrons. Electrons have a negative **charge** of electricity, and protons have a positive charge. (Neutrons have no charge.) Opposite charges attract, so when materials rub together and one material becomes negatively charged (has more electrons) and one is positively charged (has more protons), static electricity results.

When pieces of ice inside thunderclouds knock against each other, they build up an electrical charge. This can make a spark that suddenly jumps toward Earth as a flash of lightning.

Eureka moment!

In 1752, the American statesman and scientist Benjamin Franklin flew a kite in a thunderstorm to prove that lightning was a form of electricity. Lightning struck the kite, and electricity flowed down its string into a key at the end. A spark jumped across to Franklin's hand, giving him a slight shock. He was lucky. Never fly kites in storms, because the electrical charge could kill you!

Making electricity

The electricity we use at home does not come from nature. It is made in **power stations**. We make electricity by converting other sources of energy. Many power stations burn coal to boil water and produce steam. The steam hits the blades of a **turbine**, which is like a big fan. The turbine spins and rotates coils of wire that are surrounded by big **magnets**. As the wire spins, the magnets push and pull electrons in the wire. The electrons in the wire move from atom to atom to form an **electric current** that flows through the wire, like water flowing through a hose.

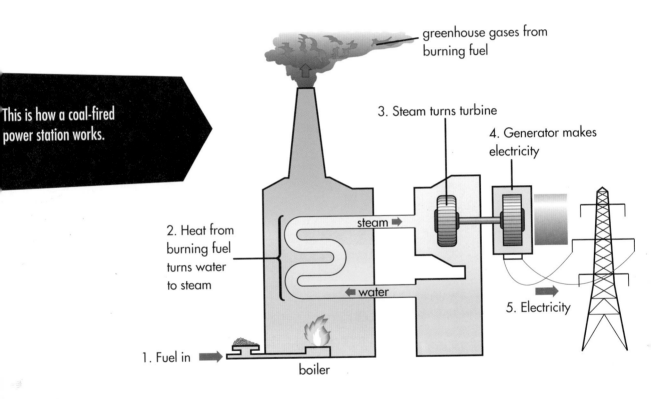

This is how a coal-fired power station works.

greenhouse gases from burning fuel

3. Steam turns turbine

4. Generator makes electricity

2. Heat from burning fuel turns water to steam

steam ➡

⬅ water

5. Electricity

1. Fuel in ➡

boiler

Eureka moment!

Michael Faraday (1791–1867) discovered that moving a magnet inside a wire coil could make electricity, and he went on to create the first electric **generator**, called the dynamo.

Electricity without coal

Other sources of energy can also be used to produce electricity. Some power stations burn natural gas to heat water and make steam to turn the turbines. A nuclear power station splits apart atoms of a metal called uranium to release heat energy. Electricity can also be produced from **renewable** sources of energy, such as wind and water. A wind farm uses the wind to spin the blades of the turbine, and a hydroelectric power station uses running or falling water.

Around one-fifth of the world's electricity is produced by moving water that spins turbines in hydroelectric power stations like this one.

How does electricity get to us?

When electricity flows out of a power station, it passes into a **transformer**. This machine increases the **voltage** so that the power can be pushed for long distances. Voltage is a measure of the force that makes electricity move. The high-voltage electric current travels through thick cables called transmission lines. You can see these cables stretching across the country, held up by giant metal towers called **transmission towers**.

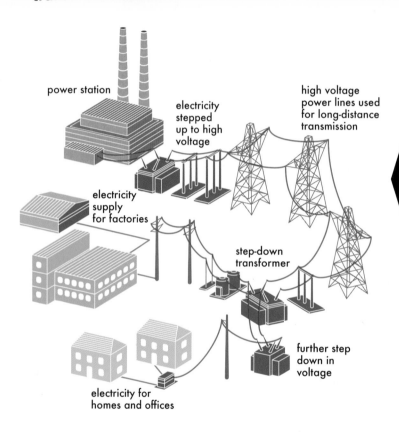

power station

electricity stepped up to high voltage

high voltage power lines used for long-distance transmission

electricity supply for factories

step-down transformer

further step down in voltage

electricity for homes and offices

The network of transformers, substations, and overhead and underground wires that delivers electricity from power stations to buildings is called the electricity grid.

WHAT'S NEXT?

To meet its target for producing 20 percent of the country's electricity from wind energy by 2030, the United States will be building many more wind-powered turbines out at sea. This will mean laying more underwater cables to carry the electricity to shore.

From transmission tower to home

When electricity cables get close to a town or city, they travel through a substation. Transformers in the substation lower the voltage so that it can pass along smaller overhead or underground power lines to the outsides of buildings. There, smaller transformers reduce the voltage again to make it the correct level for use in homes and offices.

Electricity flows into buildings through a meter that measures how much electricity people use. Wires from a meter box run through the walls of buildings to where electricity is used to power lights and other machinery.

DID YOU KNOW?

There are over 500,000 miles (about 800,000 kilometers) of transmission lines throughout the United States. Many hundreds of thousands more miles of distribution lines carry electricity to homes and offices.

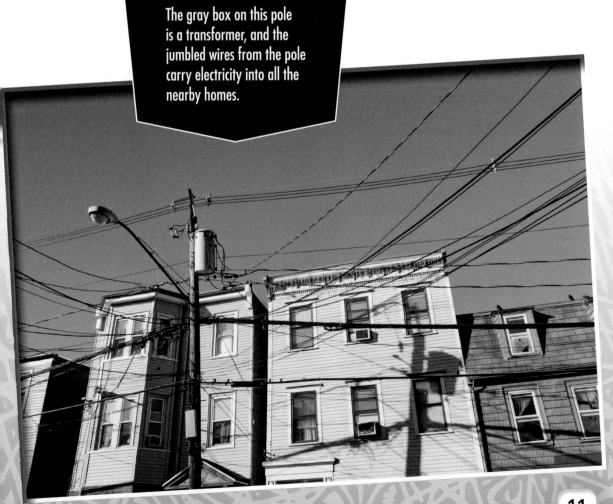

The gray box on this pole is a transformer, and the jumbled wires from the pole carry electricity into all the nearby homes.

How Do Batteries Work?

Power stations have to make and supply electricity to the grid 24 hours per day because they cannot store enough electricity to power large machines. However, batteries can store smaller amounts of electrical energy in the form of chemicals.

We use batteries to power portable machines such as flashlights. Switching on a battery-powered flashlight starts **chemical reactions** inside the battery. The reactions move electrons. An electric current flows out of one end of the battery, through the bulb to light it up, and back into the other end of the battery.

Eureka moment!

Alessandro Volta made the first working battery in 1800 from a giant stack of discs of zinc and copper separated by cardboard soaked in salt water. The metals reacted with the salt water. During this process, electrons moved from the zinc to the copper, making an electric current. We get the term *voltage* from Volta's name.

Batteries only produce small amounts of electricity, but they are ideal for powering small, portable devices such as this remote-controlled car.

Losing and gaining power

The chemical reactions inside disposable batteries weaken as they react and change into other chemicals. Eventually, they stop altogether, and we say the battery is dead. In rechargeable batteries, the chemical reactions inside can run in reverse. The chemicals take in electrons from a charger and change back to their original state.

DID YOU KNOW?

You should never throw used batteries in the trash, because the chemicals can seep out and **pollute** the environment. Collect them and make sure they are taken to a recycling center for safe disposal.

Car batteries can be recharged and reused for years. They contain large stores of acid that reacts with lead. Driving a car recharges the battery. This changes the chemicals back to their original state, so the battery can be used again and again.

Try this!

Did you know that you could turn a lemon into a battery? Try this experiment to find out how to do it!

Prediction

It is possible to change the chemical energy in a lemon into electrical energy.

What you need

- Copper wire (18-gauge wire is best; buy it from a hardware store or craft store)
- Wire clippers
- A steel paper clip
- A sheet of coarse sandpaper
- A lemon

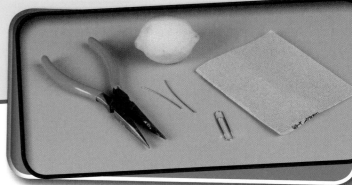

What you do

1. With the help of an adult, cut a 2-inch (5-centimeter) piece of copper wire with the clippers. (If your copper wire has plastic around it, ask an adult to help you strip the plastic off.)

2. Straighten out the steel paper clip. With the help of an adult, cut a 2-inch (5-centimeter) piece from the straightened paper clip.

3. Use the sandpaper to smooth off any rough edges on the ends of your two pieces of wire.

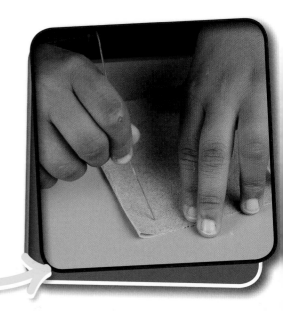

(4) Squeeze the lemon gently with your hands or roll it on a table with a flat hand to release the juices inside it. (Don't break the lemon's skin.)

(5) Push the two wires into the lemon so they are as close together as they can be without touching each other.

(6) Make your tongue wet with spit. Touch the tip of your wet tongue on the ends of the two wires. What do you feel?

Conclusion
You should be able to feel a slight tingle on your tongue! The juice in the lemon reacts differently with the steel wire and the copper wire. These two chemical reactions push electrons through the wires. Because the two metals are different, the electrons get pushed harder in one direction than the other. This current flows through your tongue when you touch the wires.

How Does Electricity Move?

Electricity needs to move in a circuit. An electrical circuit is like a pathway, usually made of wires that electric current can flow through. The word *circuit* **comes from the word** *circle*, **because electricity flows in a circular path, or loop.**

A battery or other power source pushes electrons through the wire to the device we want to power. This uses up some of the electrical energy carried by the electrons. For example, a lightbulb changes some of the energy into light. The electrons then go back to the power source to pick up more energy. They travel in a complete circuit. We can make a simple circuit from one battery connected by wires to a lightbulb.

The voltage produced by the battery pushes electric current around the wire in this circuit. The lightbulb lights up as the current flows through it.

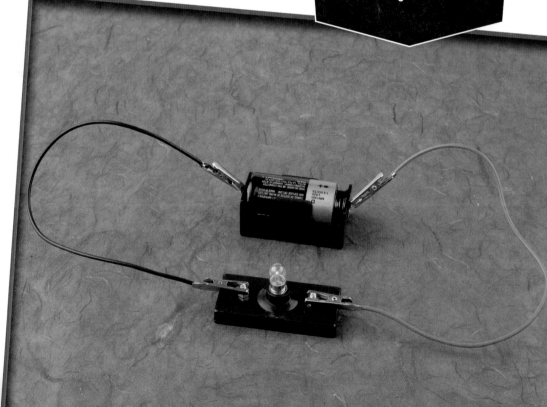

Ends of a battery

A battery has two **terminals**. These are the points from which electricity can flow or return. One terminal is positive and marked with a plus sign (+). The other is negative and marked with a minus sign (−). The electric current that flows from the battery into a wire must travel from the negative to the positive terminal to work and complete a circuit. Try turning the batteries in a flashlight or radio the other way around and see what happens!

DID YOU KNOW?

Electric eels work like a battery. The head is like the positive terminal of the battery, while the tail is like the negative terminal. When electric eels touch a fish, they can release enough electricity to kill it!

A racetrack like this one is sometimes called a circuit, meaning a continuous loop. In an electrical circuit, the path for an electric current is a continuous loop of wire.

Switches

Switches allow us to turn circuits on and off. A switch works by making or closing a gap in the circuit. When a switch is turned on, the circuit is complete. The electric current can flow through wires to power devices such as lightbulbs. When a switch is turned off, a gap is created so that the electric current cannot flow around the circuit.

Switches act like a movable bridge. When the bridge is up, there is a gap in the road and the traffic cannot move. When the bridge is down, the gap in the road is filled, and the traffic can move along it again.

We use switches many times a day to turn on lights, computers, and many other machines—but have you ever thought about how they work?

Eureka moment!

Thomas Alva Edison invented the first long-lasting lightbulb in 1879. It glowed for 13½ hours before going out. Modern, energy-saving lightbulbs can last for up to 10,000 hours.

Switched on and off

There are many different types of switches, but most consist of two metal strips with a **spring** between them. In the "on" position, the metal strips are pushed together to complete the circuit and allow the electric current to flow. In the "off" position, the spring pushes the metal strips apart to create a gap in the circuit. Switches make appliances easy to use and longer lasting. If a machine is left on, its parts wear out sooner.

WHAT'S NEXT?

In the future, we will not have to press a switch to turn on our laptops—we will be able to control them with our voices! Manufacturers believe that one day soon we will simply have to say "Log on now" to operate a switch and make computers work.

You can make a simple circuit using a paper clip to connect two wires. (The electricity flows through the wire paper clip, too.) If you move the paper clip to make a gap in the circuit, the bulb will not light up. Is this switch on or off?

Circuit symbols

Instead of drawing large, complicated pictures of electrical circuits, we can use symbols to draw circuit diagrams. The diagram does not show exactly where things are in a real-life circuit—just how the **components** of the circuit are connected together.

Circuit diagrams are also useful for explaining how electrical circuits work. People use them when designing or testing real circuits. For example, the diagrams help engineers know where to put the circuit components in a new building or machine.

DID YOU KNOW?

The same circuit symbols are used in most parts of the world, which means that everyone can understand them, no matter what language they speak.

These are some of the circuit symbols that people use. In the battery symbol, the long line represents the positive terminal and the short line represents the negative terminal.

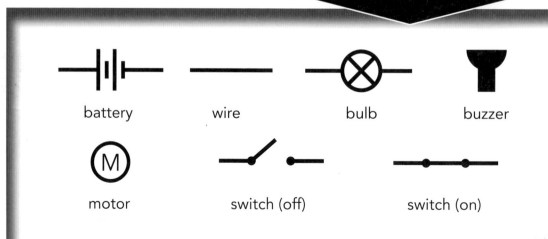

battery   wire   bulb   buzzer

motor   switch (off)   switch (on)

Circuit diagrams are helpful because describing circuits in words can be tricky and take a long time. Look at the picture below of the circuit diagram of a flashlight. We could say, "Put three batteries into the flashlight, each with the positive terminal facing the bulb and the negative terminal facing the end of the flashlight. The negative terminal is connected to the switch by wire and then that wire goes to a bulb to light it up before returning to the positive terminal at the other end of the set of batteries." Can you see how circuit diagrams are an easier way to describe this?

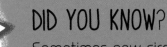
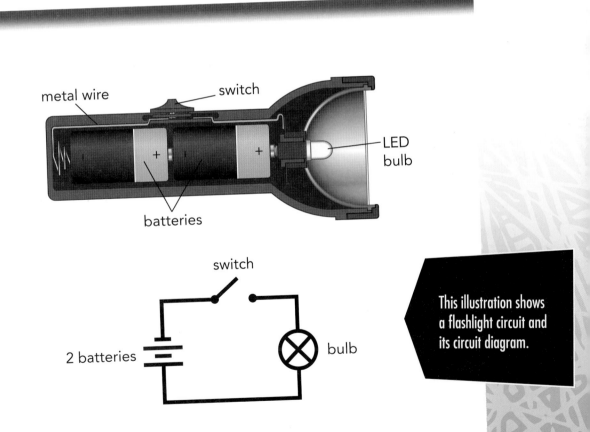

metal wire

switch

LED bulb

batteries

switch

2 batteries

bulb

This illustration shows a flashlight circuit and its circuit diagram.

How do we change circuits?

We can change circuits in various ways. Adding a battery to a simple circuit with one lightbulb will increase the voltage and make electricity flow faster. This will make the bulb brighter, because devices work harder when more electricity goes through them. If we add another bulb to a simple circuit with just one battery, both bulbs will light up, but they will be dimmer.

When two or more bulbs are added to a circuit in a line, it is called a **series circuit**. This is how bulbs are joined together on a string of lights. If one lightbulb is unscrewed, the others go out. If extra wires are added to connect extra bulbs, it is called a **parallel circuit**. This is how the lights in a house are wired together. If one bulb is unscrewed, the others stay lit up.

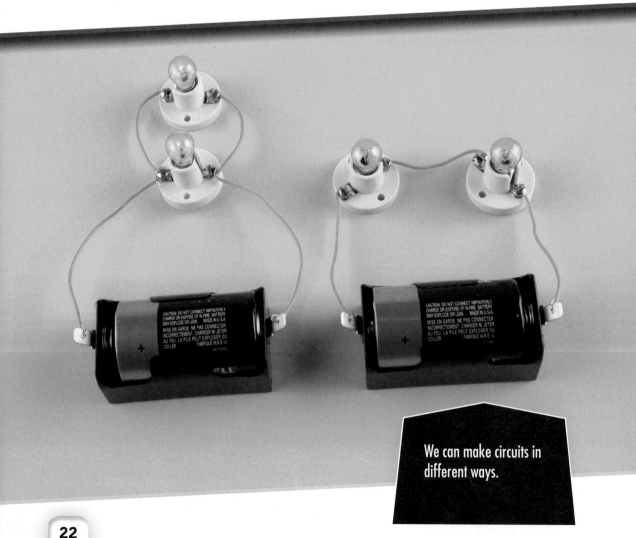

We can make circuits in different ways.

Reducing the flow

We can also change circuits by changing the length and thickness of wires. Think of a wire as a hose and the electric current as water flowing through it. It takes longer to fill a bucket with water using a thin hose than by using a thicker one of the same length. This is because the long, thin one allows less water to flow through it at once. In the same way, a long, thin wire reduces the flow of an electric current through a circuit. This is called **resistance**.

Resistance is used in various ways. For example, a dimmer switch can control the brightness of an electric light by changing the resistance in the wire in a circuit. When the resistance is greater, the light is dimmer.

DID YOU KNOW?

Electrical wire comes in different, numbered sizes. The numbers are based on electrical resistance, which increases as the wire gets thinner. Thicker wires cause less resistance, so they have a lower number.

A longer or thinner wire reduces the flow of electric current in a circuit and makes a lightbulb shine less brightly.

What Can Electricity Flow Through?

The electricity we use flows through metal wires. That is because metal is a good **conductor** of electricity. An electrical conductor is a material that has low resistance and lets electricity flow through it easily. Most metals are good conductors of electricity, but other materials can conduct electricity, too. Graphite, which is used to make some pencil leads, conducts electricity. So do concrete and water.

DID YOU KNOW?

Lightning tries to find the quickest route to the ground, so it often strikes tall buildings. Some tall buildings have metal lightning rods on their roofs. The rods are connected to wires that conduct the electricity into the ground and keep the building safe.

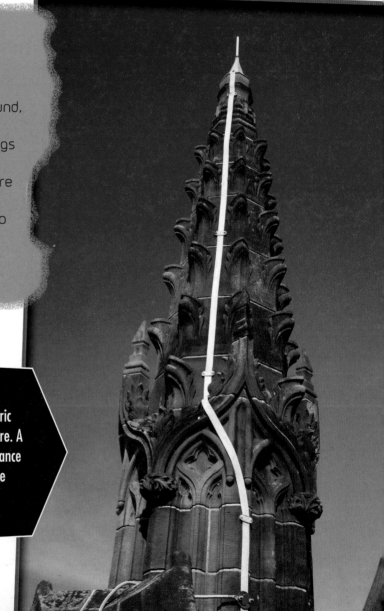

Lightning is an incredibly hot electric current that can set buildings on fire. A lightning rod is made of low-resistance metal that conducts lightning to the ground instead.

Metal conductors

Different metals conduct electricity in different ways. Silver is the best electrical conductor, and aluminum is one of the worst. However, silver is too expensive to be used in everyday electrical items, such as plugs—so copper, which is also a good conductor, is often used instead. The copper pins in plugs conduct electricity from the wall socket, through the plug, and into appliances such as computers or televisions.

Eureka moment!

In 1911, the Dutch scientist Heike Kamerlingh Onnes discovered superconductors. These are materials that allow electricity to flow through them without any resistance at all. He found that cooling the metal mercury down to extremely cold temperatures drastically reduces its electrical resistance.

Copper is a good conductor of electricity, so copper wire is often used to carry electricity into our homes and appliances.

Insulators

Insulators are the opposite of conductors. These materials have a very high resistance to electricity. Insulators conduct very little electric current and effectively block the flow of electricity. Most nonmetals are insulators. Some, such as rubber, glass, ceramics, and plastic, are particularly good insulators. Insulators are very useful for protecting objects and living things (like us!) from dangerous electric currents.

DID YOU KNOW?

Red fire ants are sensitive to (and attracted to) the charges in electrical wires. They cause expensive damage in some places because they eat insulation material to get to the wires—and then so many get electrocuted that their bodies can block switches!

Electrical workers wear protective gear made from special insulating fabrics that block the electric currents from power lines.

Insulating for safety

A thin layer of plastic covers the copper wires that carry the electric current from wall sockets into the appliances in our homes. This is an insulator that protects people from touching the live electrical wires. The electrical current cannot get through the plastic, so it is forced to follow the path of the copper wire to where the electricity is needed.

The overhead power lines that are supported by transmission towers are not covered in insulating material. However, ceramic or glass insulators are fitted between the transmission towers and the wires. This stops electricity from flowing down the metal transmission towers to the ground, where it could hurt—or even kill—people or animals.

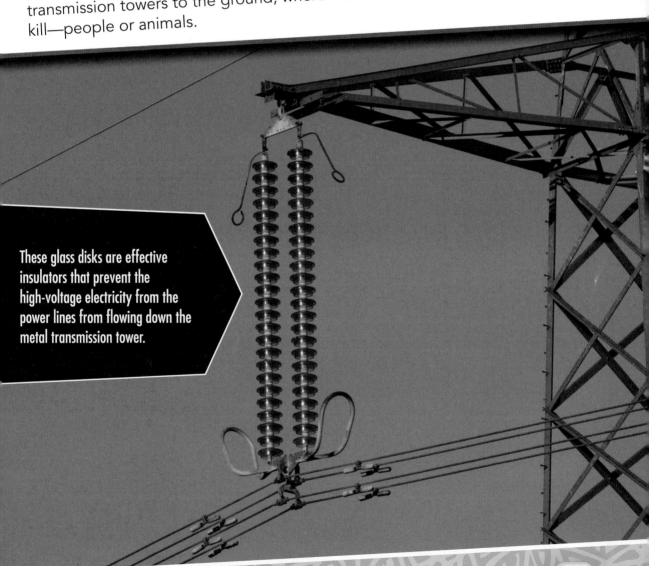

These glass disks are effective insulators that prevent the high-voltage electricity from the power lines from flowing down the metal transmission tower.

Try this!

Test out some different materials to find out which are the best conductors and insulators of electricity.

What you need

- Six different materials, such as a cork, a metal spoon, a plastic comb or spoon, a piece of aluminum foil, a glass marble, or a pencil (with both ends sharpened)
- Three pieces of plastic-coated copper wire, each about 4 inches (10 centimeters) long, with ends bare

- AA battery
- A lightbulb
- Sticky tape
- A wooden clothespin
- Two brass paper fasteners

What you do

1 Examine each of the six materials you are investigating. Which materials do you think will be good conductors? Which will be good insulators?

2 Attach a piece of wire to the positive (+) terminal of the battery, using sticky tape. Attach the other end of the wire to the side of the bulb using the clothespin. This will also allow the bulb to stand up.

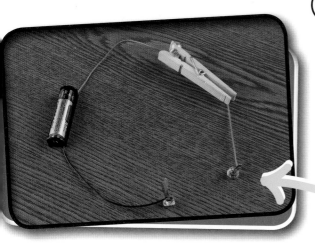

3 Attach one end of a second piece of wire to the bottom of the bulb with tape. Twist the other end of the wire around one of the paper fasteners.

4 Attach the third piece of wire to the negative (–) terminal of the battery using sticky tape. Twist the other end of the wire around the other paper fastener.

5 To test your circuit, touch the paper clips together, holding just the insulated wire. Then test the objects. Put them one at a time in the circuit between the paper fasteners, making sure they touch and have a good connection. (Remember: For a circuit to be complete, all components in the circuit must make contact.)

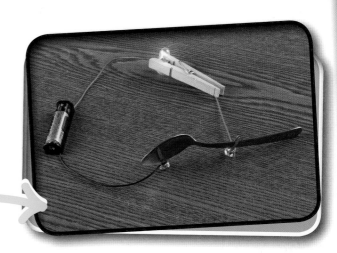

Conclusion

The materials that conduct electricity best are the ones that make the lightbulb shine more brightly. Were all your metal materials good conductors? Did different metals have different strengths of conductivity? Test other materials to see whether they can conduct electricity or insulate from it.

How Do We Use Electricity?

We can make electricity work for us because it is possible to change one type of energy to another. For example, by using electricity to power heaters, lamps, buzzers, and washing machines, we can change electrical energy into heat, light, sound, and movement energy.

When electricity is forced through a high-resistance material, the electrical energy can change into another form of energy, such as heat. Kettles and hair dryers are good examples of this process.

DID YOU KNOW?

When electricity travels long distances along cables from power stations to our homes, resistance causes up to two-thirds of its original power to escape into the air as heat. People are trying to invent lower-resistance cables, to prevent this power loss.

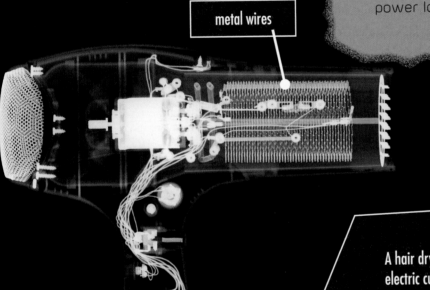

metal wires

A hair dryer gets hot because the electric current is restricted in loops of long, thin metal wires. When the electrons are forced to move through the loops, some of the electrical energy is converted into heat.

We use electricity in different ways to create light. In traditional lightbulbs, thin loops of wire made from high-resistance metal, called filaments, slow down the flow of electric current. This makes the wire so hot that it glows and produces light. Energy-efficient lightbulbs are made of tubes that are sprayed inside with a special material that can glow. When electricity flows through this coating, it glows and the bulb lights up.

Eureka moment!

Two British scientists, William Ramsay and Morris W. Travers, discovered neon in the atmosphere in 1898. Neon is a rare, colorless, odorless gas that can also be found in gases trapped in the earth. Neon gas is an excellent conductor of electricity. Neon lights are tubes filled with neon gas that glows very brightly when electricity passes through it. Stores and theaters use them in special lamps for signs on their buildings.

Electricity and magnetism

In a power-station generator, magnetism makes electricity—but electricity can make magnetism, too. When an electric current flows through a wire, it creates an invisible force of energy all around it called a **magnetic field**. To make the magnetic field stronger, wire can be wound into a tight coil around an iron bar. The combined magnetic field of all the turns of wire passes through the center of the coil and makes an **electromagnet**. Unlike a normal bar magnet, an electromagnet is temporary, because it stops working when the electric current is turned off.

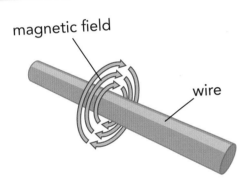

magnetic field

wire

An electric current runs through a single wire, generating a weak magnetic field.

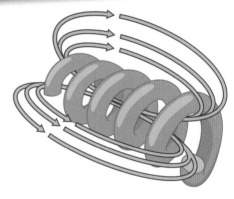

When the wire is wound into a coil, it concentrates the magnetic field and makes it stronger. More electrical current will produce an even stronger field.

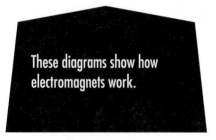

These diagrams show how electromagnets work.

DID YOU KNOW?

The huge metal plates at the end of cranes that are used to lift cars in a scrap yard or to sort metal at a recycling center are actually electromagnets!

Using electromagnets

We can use electromagnets to convert electric energy into sound energy. Sound is the energy that things produce when they **vibrate**. When you press a doorbell, an electromagnet pulls an iron rod so that it hits a metal bell. This makes the bell vibrate and produce a "ding" sound. A buzzer works in a similar way, but the rod moves dozens of times per second to make the buzzing sound.

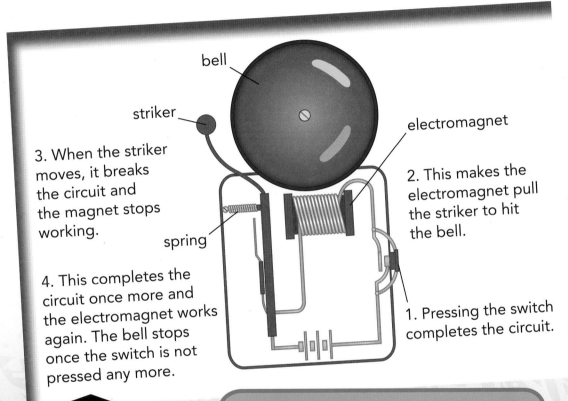

bell

striker

electromagnet

3. When the striker moves, it breaks the circuit and the magnet stops working.

spring

2. This makes the electromagnet pull the striker to hit the bell.

4. This completes the circuit once more and the electromagnet works again. The bell stops once the switch is not pressed any more.

1. Pressing the switch completes the circuit.

When you push a doorbell, you complete an electrical circuit that powers an electromagnet that makes a striker hit the bell. The movement breaks the circuit, the striker moves away from the bell, and the process starts again.

WHAT'S NEXT?

Some people believe that more countries around the world will use high-speed maglev trains in the future. (*Maglev* is short for "magnetic levitation.") Maglev trains use electromagnets to hover above the rails and can travel at speeds of up to 270 miles (430 kilometers) per hour!

Try this!

Make a simple electromagnet and turn it on and off, to see how it is only magnetic when electricity is flowing.

What you need

- A large iron nail, about 2½ inches (6 centimeters) long
- About 3½ feet (1 meter) of plastic-coated copper wire
- A new D-size battery
- A D-size battery holder
- Some paper clips

What you do

1 Wrap most of the wire around the nail, leaving about 10 inches (15 centimeters) of loose wire at both ends. Try not to overlap the wire as you coil it around the nail.

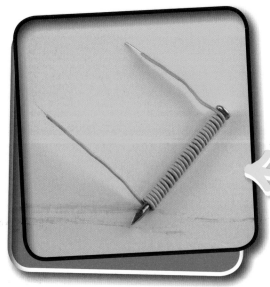

(2) With an adult's help, remove about 1 inch (2.5 centimeters) of plastic coating from both ends of the wire. Attach one end of the wire to one end of the battery, and the other end of the wire to the other end of the battery. If you don't have a battery holder, you can use sticky tape to do this—but be careful, because the wire can get hot.

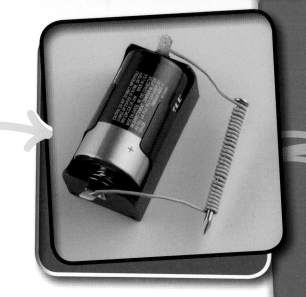

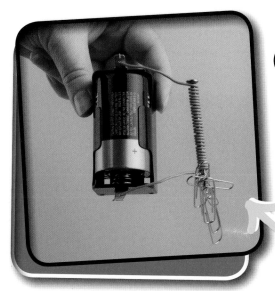

(3) Hold the middle part of the nail, where the electrical wire is coiled. Then move the tip of the nail near the paper clips and see if it will pick them up.

Conclusion

If the nail picks up the paper clips, you have made an electromagnet! You could also see if the number of times you wrap the wire around the nail affects the strength of the electromagnet. Does the thickness or length of the nail affect the electromagnet's strength? Does the thickness of the wire affect the power of the electromagnet?

Stay safe!

An electromagnet uses up battery power quite quickly and the battery may get warm, so disconnect the wires as soon as you have finished the experiment. And *never* put the wires of the electromagnet near a household electrical socket.

Electric motors

An electric motor uses electromagnets to create motion. All magnets have a north pole and a south pole. The end points to where their magnetic power is strongest. The rule with magnets is that opposite poles attract and same poles repel, or push each other away. So, if you have two magnets, two north poles will repel each other, as will two south poles. But when a north pole of one is close to the south pole of another, they attract each other.

Inside an electric motor, an electromagnet is placed inside a circular magnet. When a current passes through the electromagnet, its magnetic field pushes and pulls against the magnetic field of the permanent magnet. This makes the electromagnet and the connected parts of a machine spin.

The motor in a blender turns a blade that mixes or beats the food.

Motorized machines

We use electric motors to work many different kinds of electric machines. In fact, almost anything that moves in an electric machine uses an electric motor. An electric motor spins the drum in a clothes washing machine. In a dishwasher, an electric motor powers the pump that forces water up into the arms that spray water on the dishes. A CD player uses an electric motor to spin CDs, and an electric motor moves wiper blades back and forth across a car windshield.

WHAT'S NEXT?

We may all be driving electric cars in the future. These cars will be smaller, because electric motors are smaller than gasoline engines. They will use less energy to run— and may even be able to reduce the number of collisions by, for example, warning drivers about possible hazards and communicating with other cars.

An electric car is powered by an electric motor rather than a gasoline engine.

Zero Emi

Is Electricity Safe?

Electricity is incredibly useful, and it is safe if we use and handle it properly. We can handle batteries because they have a low or small voltage. But electricity coming from an outlet is much more powerful and can be dangerous.

We have devices called **circuit breakers** to ensure the electric current that passes into our homes is at a safe level. A circuit breaker is fitted into the supply panel where power cables enter a building. They break the circuit and stop electricity from coming into the building if the current suddenly gets too strong. Circuit breakers usually work by using an electromagnet that gets stronger as the current increases and eventually separates parts of the circuit to break it.

Fuses

A fuse inside a plug is a circuit breaker, too. A fuse is a thin, high-resistance wire. If the electricity flowing through a plug suddenly becomes too powerful (for example, if lightning strikes the building), the fuse melts. This breaks the circuit and stops the extra electricity from flowing into an appliance and starting a fire. To make the appliance work again, we have to put in a new fuse.

Electrical appliances such as this toaster can catch fire if their wires get too hot. This can happen if a current that is larger than expected passes through them or the wires are damaged.

Electric current is measured in units called **amps**. If a fuse is labeled 5 amps, then an electric current greater than 5 amps will melt the fuse. It is important to use the correct fuse for each plug.

DID YOU KNOW?

Science teacher Andre Marie Ampere (1775–1836) built the first instrument for measuring the flow of electric current. That is why we measure electric current in units called amps.

Each plug has a fuse inside it that will break the circuit if too much electric current flows through it.

fuse

Safety tips

You have to be very careful with electricity, because it can give you an electric shock. This happens when electricity passes through a human body. An electric shock can just give you a nasty jolt, but it can also cause serious burns, or even death, so it is important to know how to keep safe.

The overhead transmission lines and power lines that distribute electricity to our homes are not insulated, because they are high above the ground and out of reach. They carry high-voltage electric current, so they are very dangerous. If you touch them, or touch anything else that can conduct electric current from them to you, you could get an electric shock. You should never climb a transmission tower, electricity pole, or trees growing close to or around power lines. Be very careful after a storm, because power lines may have been blown down to the ground.

Always fly kites in wide-open spaces, far away from power lines. If a kite touches an overhead power line, the current could travel down the kite string and hurt you.

Indoor safety

Never touch anything electrical with wet hands or take electrical appliances into bathrooms. Water could conduct the electric current to you and give you a shock. Never use or touch an appliance with a damaged cable. If you touch the wire beneath the damaged plastic insulation, you will get a shock. Finally, never put too many plugs into an adaptor plug. This can cause too much electric current to flow through the socket and start a fire.

DID YOU KNOW?

Human bodies are made up of two-thirds water—which makes us good conductors of electricity! If you touch an electric current, it spreads through the water in your body and gives you an electric shock.

Firefighters use special powders to put out electrical fires. Using water could conduct the electricity to the firefighters and give them an electric shock.

Electricity in the Future

Most of the electricity that people use around the world is made by burning **fossil fuels** such as coal, gas, and oil. Fossil fuels got their name because they formed from the remains of living things that died millions of years ago. The fact that fossil fuels take so long to form means we cannot replace them and they are gradually running out.

Another problem with fossil fuels is that burning them releases gases such as carbon dioxide into the air, and this helps to hold heat in Earth's atmosphere. Most scientists believe that burning fossil fuels is contributing to **global warming**.

Global warming is an increase in the world's average temperatures. This increase in heat is melting the ice in the Arctic and Antarctic and can cause forest fires and drought conditions like those seen here in Kenya, Africa.

Cleaner electricity

One way to reduce the amount of fossil fuels we use is for governments to invest more money in renewable sources of energy, such as solar, wind, and water power. These types of energy do not release **greenhouse gases** into the atmosphere and will not run out.

Individuals can make a difference, too. For example, we can choose to buy machines and appliances that use less electricity, such as energy-efficient lightbulbs and washing machines. We can turn off lights and other electrical items when we are not using them and keep doors and windows closed when the central heating or air conditioning is turned on.

The winds are stronger higher up in the sky, so some wind-energy generators are built like giant kites and conduct electricity to Earth through long wires. Perhaps we will see more of these in the sky in the future.

DID YOU KNOW?

Leaving just six electrical devices on "standby" is the same as leaving a 60-watt lightbulb on for the same amount of time—and can increase a household's energy bills by nearly one-fifth!

Glossary

amber hardened tree resin. (Resin is the sticky juice that flows from beneath a tree's bark.)

amp unit used to measure electric current

atom smallest part of a substance that can take part in a chemical reaction

charge when something is electrically charged, it has electricity in it

chemical reaction when the atoms in different things react with each other and change

circuit complete path or loop along which electric current flows from a power source and back again

circuit breaker device that can stop an electric current from flowing if it becomes dangerous

component part of an electric circuit. Batteries, wires, and bulbs can be components.

conductor material that allows electricity to move easily through it

electric current flow or movement of electricity

electromagnet magnet that only works when an electric current passes through it

electron very small part of an atom, with a negative electric charge

energy force that we need to move and grow; machines also need energy to work

fossil fuel fuel such as coal or oil that was formed from plants or animals that died millions of years ago

generator machine that converts mechanical energy into electrical energy

global warming gradual rise in the temperature of Earth's atmosphere

greenhouse gas gas such as carbon dioxide that helps to hold heat in the atmosphere

magnet object or material that creates pushing or pulling forces that can attract or repel (push away) some other objects or materials and other magnets

magnetic field invisible area around a magnet or electromagnet that contains the active force of magnetism

neutron very small part of an atom, with no electric charge

parallel circuit circuit in which the current divides into two or more paths before meeting up again to complete the circuit

pollute add dirty, harmful, or dangerous substances to air, water, or soil

power station factory where electricity is made

proton very small part of an atom, with a positive electric charge

renewable can be used without running out

resistance measure of how an object restricts the flow of current

series circuit circuit in which the current goes through all its parts or components one after the other

spring tightly coiled metal wire that can be crushed or stretched, but always returns to its original shape

static electricity type of energy that is made when something has too many electrons or protons

terminal point at which connections can be made in an electric circuit

transformer device for increasing or reducing the voltage of an electrical power supply

transmission tower tall, metal tower that carries electricity cables high above the ground

turbine machine that is powered by pressure from steam, water, or wind

vibrate move up and down or back and forth

voltage amount of electrical force that makes electricity move through a wire. We measure this force in volts; the bigger the voltage, the bigger the flow of electric current.

Find Out More

Books

Hewitt, Sally. *Amazing Electricity* (Amazing Science). New York: Crabtree, 2008.

Monroe, Ronald. *What Are Electrical Circuits?* (Understanding Electricity). New York: Crabtree, 2012.

Mullins, Matt. *Electricity* (True Books). New York: Children's Press, 2012.

Parker, Steve. *Energy and Power* (How It Works). Broomall, Pa.: Mason Crest, 2011.

Swanson, Jennifer. *The Shocking Truth About Electricity* (Fact Finders: Lol Physical Science). Mankato, Minn.: Capstone, 2013.

Web sites

www.eia.gov/kids/energy.cfm?page=electricity_home-basics

This web site has facts about electricity and how it is made and used.

greenliving.nationalgeographic.com/children-can-save-electricity-2757. html

This web site gives lots of tips about how to save electricity.

www.ndt-ed.org/EducationResources/HighSchool/Electricity/ workwithelectricity.htm

This interactive web site explains electricity.

www.need.org/needpdf/infobook_activities/ElemInfo/ElecE.pdf

This web site provides a recap of the definition of electricity, how it is made, and how it gets to us.

Places to visit

Exploratorium
Pier 15
San Francisco, California 94111
www.exploratorium.edu

This museum examines many different aspects of science, including electricity, and offers hands-on activities.

SPARK Museum of Electrical Invention
1312 Bay Street
Bellingham, Washington 98225
www.sparkmuseum.org

This museum features interactive exhibits that examine the history and science of electricity.

Further research

Create a timeline of electrical discoveries and inventions, starting with some of the Eureka subjects in this book.

Which uses more power—a refrigerator or a TV? Learn more about why different devices use different amounts of electricity. Find out about the energy savings made by running energy-efficient machines and changing energy use habits in your home or school.

Find out more about the differences between sources of renewable energy, from wind to solar. What are the pros and cons of each? Which type would be most suitable for the region where you live?

Index

adaptor plugs 41
aluminum 25
amber 5, 6
amps 39
appliances 19, 25, 27, 30, 36, 37, 38, 41, 43
atoms 4, 7, 8, 9

batteries 12–15, 16, 17, 20, 22, 35, 38

cars, electric 37
chemical reactions 12, 13, 15
circuit breakers 38
circuit diagrams 20–21
circuit symbols 20
circuits 16–23, 33
conductors 24–25, 28–29, 31, 41
copper 25, 27

dimmer switches 23
doorbells 33
dynamos 8

electric currents 8, 10, 12, 15, 16, 17, 18, 23, 24, 26, 27, 30, 31, 32, 38, 39, 40, 41
electric eels 17
electric shocks 40, 41
electrical energy 4, 5, 8, 9, 16, 30, 33
electricity grid 10, 12
electromagnets 32, 33, 34–35, 36, 38
electrons 4, 5, 6, 7, 8, 12, 13, 15, 16
energy conversion 8, 30, 33
energy-efficient appliances 18, 31, 43
experiments 14–15, 28–29, 34–35

filaments 31
fossil fuels 42, 43
fuses 38, 39

generators 8
global warming 42
graphite 24
greenhouse gases 43

heat energy 9, 30
hydroelectricity 9

insulators 26–27, 28–29

kite flying 7, 40

lemon battery 14–15
light 31
lightbulbs 12, 16, 18, 19, 22, 23, 28–29, 31, 43
lightning 6, 7, 24, 38
lightning rods 24

maglev trains 33
magnetic fields 32, 36
magnetism 8, 32–35, 36, 38
mercury 25
metals 15, 19, 24, 25, 32
motors, electric 36–37

negative charge 7
neon 31
neutrons 4, 7
north and south poles 36

parallel circuits 22
plastic 26, 27, 41
plugs 25, 38, 39, 41
pollution 13
positive charge 7
power cuts 5
power lines 10, 11, 26, 27, 40

power stations 8, 9, 10, 12, 32
protective clothing 26
protons 4, 7

red fire ants 26
renewable energy 9, 10, 43
resistance 23, 24, 25, 26, 30, 31

safety 7, 35, 38–41
series circuits 22
silver 25
sound energy 33
standby mode 43
static electricity 6–7
substations 11
superconductors 25
switches 18–19, 23

terminals 17, 20, 21
transformers 10, 11
transmission lines 10, 11, 40
transmission towers 10, 27, 40
turbines 8, 9, 10

using electricity 30–31

vibrations 33
voltage 10, 11, 12, 15, 16, 22, 40

water 9, 10, 24, 41
wind energy 9, 10, 43
wires 15, 22, 23, 24, 26, 27, 30, 31, 32, 34–35, 38, 43